BUSINESS AND SOCIAL CHANGE

McKINSEY FOUNDATION LECTURE SERIES

Sponsored by the
Graduate School of Business, Columbia University

Blough—*Free Man and the Corporation*

Cordiner—*New Frontiers for Professional Managers*

Donner—*The World-wide Industrial Enterprise*

Folsom—*Executive Decision Making*

Greenewalt—*The Uncommon Man*

Houser—*Big Business and Human Values*

Kappel—*Vitality in a Business Enterprise*

Mortimer—*The Purposeful Pursuit of Profits and Growth in Business*

Oates—*Business and Social Change*

Rockefeller—*Creative Management in Banking*

Watson—*A Business and Its Beliefs*

BUSINESS
AND SOCIAL CHANGE

Life Insurance Looks to the Future

JAMES F. OATES, JR.

Chairman of the Board and
Chief Executive Officer
The Equitable Life Assurance Society
of the United States

McGraw-Hill Book Company

NEW YORK   SAN FRANCISCO   TORONTO   LONDON   SYDNEY

BUSINESS AND SOCIAL CHANGE

The continuing theme of the Columbia-McKinsey Lectures is the management of large organizations. It is not without significance that successive occupants of this distinguished podium have felt it appropriate to present their views of organizational policies and controls only in the light of the environment in which the organization functions. Biologists tell us that those forms of animate life that best adapt to their environment will survive and prosper. The sociologists say the same thing about the institutions and organizations that men evolve to conduct their mutual affairs. The lesson is not lost on businessmen. It may well be that this perceptive response of business leadership to the needs and aspirations of the community is the ultimate source of strength of the corporation, more so than the vast array of laws and judicial and administrative rulings that are generally thought to provide the sanction.

No business is more sensitive to its environment than life insurance. At the same time, there is a reciprocal realization among leaders of this business that the response to environmental changes is not without its effects upon those changes. In these lectures, the twelfth in the series presented by the Columbia Graduate School of Business and supported by the McKinsey Foundation for Management Research, Mr. James F. Oates, Jr., the chairman and chief executive officer of the Equitable Life Assurance Society of the United States, has given us a vivid case history of adaptation in action.

Humanism has long been conceived of as the primary concern of the theologian, or perhaps of the government man. If a concern of business at all, it was thought to come not through business itself but through an institution created as a counterpoise to business—the labor union. Yet we learn from these lectures that the very development of life insurance as a unique service of our times has resulted from an early recognition by businessmen of an urgent and personal need of individuals to secure themselves against the emerging hazards of a society becoming more complex. More than half a century passed before government recognized that population growth and urbanization create risks that can be covered only through group action.

Today the provision of security is a bifurcated task shared by government and business, with the former providing a broadly extended floor of protection and the latter a wide variety of additional and imaginative coverages built upon that floor. But it was business that first recognized the human needs of a changing environment, initiated programs adapted to those needs, and made the individual aware that the means of meeting his needs are available.

The essential raison d'être of the life insurance business is to provide individuals with protection against hazards through the pooling of a part of their resources. The employment of those resources in the work of the community provides another opportunity to serve the needs of a changing environment. In these lectures, Mr. Oates describes how the investment policies of the life insurance companies have shifted as the needs of the time have been modified. At one time railroad bonds predominated in the portfolios—then public utilities. In the two world wars the insurance companies contributed importantly to the development of a government bond market. Concomitantly, the expansion of farms and the building of homes was facilitated by the increased holdings of real estate mortgages. At present the need for community development and redevelopment is assuming prominence as a potential employer of the pooled resources of the insured. Ways must and no doubt will be found to protect the resources as well as to use them for this latest need of a changing environment.

Many different kinds of talents must be enlisted and coordinated in the administrative structure of a life insurance organization if it is to remain an adaptive, flexible entity. Actuaries, salesmen, and investment analysts must be supplemented with cultural anthropologists and other behavioral scientists if present trends are to be projected accurately into future societal patterns. With the introduction of rapid data processing, computer technicians and programmers must be woven into the fabric of the personnel, as clerical adjustments are made to accommodate the new information technology. Above all, there must be a perceptive and imaginative leader. One cannot leave these lectures without an awareness that Mr. James F. Oates, Jr. has supplied that cohesive talent.

Courtney C. Brown
Dean, Graduate School of Business
Columbia University

CONTENTS

1

ON MEETING HUMAN NEEDS

INTRODUCTION

I suspect that no business enterprise—irrespective of size or type—has ever survived and prospered which failed to take account of the necessary interplay between near-term and long-term considerations. An exclusive concern with immediate outcomes has typically proved to be just as fatal as compulsive preoccupation with the potential rewards of an illusory future. Consequently, I believe it is implicit in sound management theory that simultaneous attention be given to the present and the future.

But the purpose of these Columbia-McKinsey Lectures is not so much to develop new knowledge as it is to show how the principles, which have been applied in one type of business enterprise, might contribute to the success of other types.

Some Assumptions

An underlying theme of these lectures—serving social change—commends itself to me since it rests

2

upon three assumptions which seem particularly applicable to the life insurance business today. These are that (1) every business enterprise operates to meet human needs through the use of capital; (2) human needs change as social values change; and (3) businesses succeed to the degree that the changes in social values are recognized and the resulting new or changed human needs identified and served.

Human Needs and Capital. Our business, life insurance, is a prime example of how human needs are met through the use of capital. It is a social instrument in both its insuring and its investing functions. In providing immediate and continuing protection, it is dedicated to enhancing the worth of the individual. This, of course, requires the recognition and close observance of changing human needs. In providing capital, it assumes the vast and long-range reciprocal responsibility of serving the society within which individuals live. Life insurance thus performs the dual human service of providing security for the individual and nourishment for the economy.

Changing Needs. We are not dealing, however,

with a static relationship. As human needs and social values change in the course of a lifetime, man's
need for security not only evolves but man himself
reaches out to attain different and specific objectives. For some, security is the simple knowledge
that funds to cover funeral expenses have been put
aside. For others, the main concern may be for the
future welfare of a spouse. Then it may extend to
the knowledge that children and even grandchildren will be provided for. The range is great and
the combinations of objectives many: a guarantee
of funds for the education of children, provision
for old age, protection against ill health or catastrophic sickness, conservation of a business threat-
ened by the death of a partner, payment of a mortgage, and liquidity to meet taxes are examples. The
human needs which may be met by life and health
insurance touch on many of the most basic dimensions of life.

Social Change. Furthermore, needs change as
society itself changes. As people become more mobile and better educated, society tends to become
more highly industrialized and more complex in its
organization. All business enterprises adapt in

different ways to social change and, indeed, influence social change to varying degrees. Here, too, life insurance provides a dramatic illustration. It is necessarily concerned not only with each current generation but with the succeeding generation. Furthermore, through its long-term investments, it influences to some degree the form, content, and values of our national life. Such influence is inevitable, be it for good or ill.

The Present and Future. Thus the life insurance industry has long since accepted the assumption, testified to by its own experience, that both present and future time perspectives must coexist—that attention to immediate concerns is in no way inconsistent with objectives reaching far ahead. The life insurance contract (or policy) itself symbolizes this philosophy. The moment a policy is purchased, an immediate, if inchoate, estate is created with inherent obligations and commitments of continuing long-term social and financial significance. Though man's needs for immediate and existing protection may be temporally imperious, the underlying objectives—individually and in the aggregate—which are served in meeting these

5

needs have long-term and continuing significance.

This first lecture—"On Meeting Human Needs"—reviews the near-term and long-term considerations involved in serving the currently changing insurance requirements of the public. My second lecture—"On the Use of Capital"—applies the same ideas and beliefs to the investment function. The third and final lecture—"On Serving Social Change"—stresses and illustrates the vital importance of a general management philosophy which is sensitive to both present and future values.

Three Recurring Principles

Three basic convictions, it is submitted, form a frame of reference for such a philosophy. They are the guides which illuminate the problems and lead to the solutions; they provide both the procedure and the motivation for successful effort.

Concern for the Individual. First, it is believed that an essential responsibility of any business enterprise is to conduct its affairs in such a way as to maintain and enhance the worth of the individual human being. Several facets of contemporary thought profoundly underscore the significance of the individual. Certainly, the individual on the job is now regarded not as an economic man who works merely for economic ends but as an individual with values and emotional involvements of his own. He has come to be recognized as a person seeking a personal and social identity, as one who must have a view of himself not simply as an anonymous contributor to some larger whole but as a person with his own unique integrity. No longer does responsible management believe that human beings have an inherent dislike for work. We now realize that man's potential is far from circumscribed and that it is management's responsibility to see to it that the individual has every opportunity for maximum development.

The Innovating Organization. Second, it is well to remember that any type of enterprise, system, or organization must be constantly renewed if it is to survive. Management must strive for the wisdom, adaptability, and inspiration required to meet the demands of self-renewal—so necessary to embrace innovation and import new energy into the enterprise.

The Systems Approach. And finally, we should recall the basic idea that human society itself is essentially a system of interdependent parts and that a change in one part cannot occur without creating changes in the others. If one area is economically depressed or enlightened by a new sense of participation or burdened by crime and delinquency or lifted by vision and imagination or blighted by monopolistic power—then it surely follows that other parts of the society will feel the consequences. The key illustration of this principle is found in the interdependence of the public and private fields of activity. In our time, we are only beginning to recognize this necessary interdependence and to search for new bases of rapprochement and partnership. So much for our philosophical background.

In this first lecture, I shall range broadly through the somewhat complex and little known field of insurance operations as they have responded to social change and contributed to it. It is a long and intricate story. It is a story characterized by paradoxes, dilemmas, and continuing problems. It is hoped that you will find it both interesting and useful and parts of it, at least, might be generally applicable to other and quite different types of businesses.

THE NATURE OF THE INSURANCE ENTERPRISE

The insurance enterprise is basically a financial pooling operation designed to provide benefits to participants in return for contributions to the pool. As a social institution, it provides an unambiguous demonstration of the proposition that men are capable of cooperating with each other to achieve rational and mutually satisfactory ends. The contributions from the large number of participants in the pool create a fund that may be drawn upon to provide benefits to those suffering a defined loss, even if it occurs immediately after the insurance takes effect. In the case of life insurance, an immediate and continuing death benefit—typically a relatively substantial amount—is guaranteed. In the case of health insurance, the insurer guarantees to maintain income while the insured is disabled or to provide benefits to help meet hospital, surgical, and other medical expenses. The individual participant's contribution to the pool operates in two ways: (1) to pay for a portion of the benefits currently being received by others and (2) to purchase his own right to similar benefits at any time in the future when his own needs are evoked.

Insurance, in other words, is multi-dimensional. Temporally, it implies both a future and a present aspect. Functionally, it serves both the individual and society.

It is quite evident, of course, that any insurance company, in order to stay in business, must conduct its affairs so as to ensure that the benefits it pays out do not exceed the assets it acquires and generates.

The Problem of Coverage

Two broad classes of people tend, under our system, to be either underinsured or uninsured: those who are simply poor risks and those who, for whatever reason, have no interest in the future contingencies covered by insurance.

As we shall see presently, the poor risks typically are able to compensate for their statistical inadequacies by paying extra premiums or to obtain coverage by virtue of their membership in some group which is insured under a group plan.

As for the other category of people, their lack of insurance may be due to lack of knowledge, indifference, poor planning, or inadequate means. Many of the people without insurance today simply are very poor. As sociological research has repeatedly shown, one of the by-products of poverty is a constricted outlook—one in which considerations of the immediate present operate almost to the exclusion of future considerations.

The foregoing sharply reveals a paradox with which we constantly wrestle. An important strength of insurance companies lies in their ability to focus on the "normal" population and on those who have the financial ability to pay premiums. This calls attention to an important problem—the difficulty (if not the impossibility) of meeting the full spectrum of human requirements for protection. These matters will be referred to again when we consider the relationship of private insurance to public programs.

Underwriting

A life insurance company must select (or "underwrite") its risks to avoid being exposed to guar-

11

anteeing benefits for an unduly high proportion of medically impaired lives or lives which for other reasons may be expected to produce excessive rates of mortality. In the early days of life insurance, underwriting was a fairly simple procedure. After signing an application containing only a few short questions relating to excessive drinking and possibly other forms of intemperance and giving some assurance that he was not subject to any disorder which might "shorten his days," the applicant appeared in person before the insurance company's board of directors.

Needless to say, this face-to-face procedure was not destined to continue for long. As the business of life insurance expanded, the procedure necessarily became more complicated. As you fully realize, underwriting today is quite a detailed and systematic process, sometimes entailing extensive study of medical and other aspects of each risk, particularly in applications for large amounts.

The life insurance enterprise also offers protection against the financial hazards of living too long, i.e., outliving one's assets or other resources. This protection is afforded through the familiar mechanism of the annuity contract. Annuities, like life insurance, are essentially a pooling operation. In return for specified contributions by participants in the pool, each annuitant is guaranteed an income for life—those dying early and receiving less than they paid into the pool help to pay for those who live to an old age and receive much more than they paid into the pool. In general, we do not examine the health of applicants for annuities because there is obviously no incentive on the part of a person in bad health to buy an annuity. On the other hand, we can scarcely refuse to accept an applicant on the grounds that he is too healthy. An interesting sidelight is that the mortality among insured lives individually selected by the life underwriter after carefully looking into medical histories, etc., is heavier than the mortality experienced among persons buying annuities, even though the latter are not subjected to a medical examination and are not individually selected. Annuitants obviously do a pretty good job of self-selection. The very security of the guaranteed annuity may well be conducive to health and repose. I suspect that every annuitant entertains some belief in his own personal immortality.

Let us turn now to a very brief, but necessarily somewhat technical, description of the main types of insurance currently available as a basis for a common understanding of some of the problems with which we grapple.

Basic Types of Individual Life Policies

The simplest form is "yearly renewable term" which provides a level death benefit. It is a "pay-as-you-go" plan, each year's premium paying for the cost of insurance. Premiums increase each year since the rate of mortality increases with age.

A sounder approach is "level premium" insurance under which premiums in the early years are more than enough to pay for the risk, part of such early years' premiums being reserved to help pay for the increased risk in the later years.

Level premium life insurance may provide a death benefit for a fixed period of coverage (term insurance); a death benefit for the whole of life with premiums payable until death (ordinary life);

14

a death benefit for the whole of life but with premiums payable only for a specified period at the end of which the insurance is paid up and continues until the benefit is paid on death (limited payment life); payment of the benefit on death during a specified period or at end of the period if the insured is then alive (endowment).

Decreasing term insurance is a variation involving payment of a level premium for a death benefit decreasing each year or each month over the period of the coverage. It recognizes that in many family situations the insurance needs may decrease as the children grow up or as a mortgage or other debt is amortized.

The multiplicity of types of life policies developed over the years are, for the most part, variations of the basic forms described above, and each is designed to deal with specific needs. It would be interesting, if time permitted, to review in detail the several important categories of policies recently inaugurated. We take considerable satisfaction, for example, in the family policy (whole life on husband, whole life or term on wife, term [convertible] on children), in the joint life policy (on business or conjugal partners), in the option to purchase additional insurance (guaranteed insurability), in the various forms of retirement policies, and in the many forms of individual health insurance. The needs for security are varied and they are constantly changing.

EXTENSION OF COVERAGE TO BROADER SEGMENTS OF THE POPULATION

The general consequence of such innovative developments in the industry has been to make insurance available to more and more people to cover newly developing contingencies. Only twenty-five years ago there were many medical impairments which would disqualify an applicant for life insurance. In contrast, and as may not be generally known, we now accept regularly applicants with histories of heart attacks, cancer, or diabetes. In this respect, the industry's efforts to meet human needs are helpful in the public and individual interest. There are many life insurance companies that will now insure persons who are expected to experience mortality up to ten times the rate of mortality on "standard" lives—subject, of course,

16

to the payment of an extra premium to cover the additional risk.

Industrial Insurance

Although life insurance was being conducted successfully by a number of reliable companies well over a hundred years ago, it was available almost entirely to the middle- and upper-income groups, being largely out of reach of wage-earning families. Individual policies were issued only in larger amounts than these families could afford; premiums were not payable in small, frequent installments; and there was no home collection service. Wage earners were limited largely to death benefits sold by so-called "friendly fraternal societies" or "burial clubs."

To meet the demand for dependable life insurance for lower-income groups, industrial life insurance was introduced in Great Britain in 1854 and in the United States in 1875. Industrial policies were made available in face amounts of less than the $1,000 minimum prevalent for individual life insurance, premiums were payable weekly, and the agents (debitmen) called regularly at the homes of policyholders. Through this medium, the companies made available life insurance especially adapted to the needs and circumstances of these lower-income families.

The amount of industrial insurance in force rose steadily until the early 1950s but has remained relatively level for over a decade. In 1915, it represented 20 percent of the total life insurance in force; fifty years later, it had declined to 4.4 percent of such total. Although industrial insurance has probably passed its zenith, it remains an important source of life insurance coverage, particularly for women and children, in heavy industrial areas and in the South. For more than seventy years it provided a minimum floor of protection to millions of industrial workers who would not otherwise have found the protection afforded by these policies.

The Advent of Group Insurance

To omit any discussion of group insurance would obviously leave our story but half told. Let us first glance at the historical background. As the Industrial Revolution gradually altered the agricultural system that has prevailed for centuries in the Western World and accelerated the urbanization of population, men traded the often meager but certain security of the land for the glowing promises of the city. Rural independence tended to be replaced by urban interdependence. Each man contributed his special talent or skill and received in return a wage—a wage that was taken to be sufficient for the necessities of living but which often left nothing to provide for illness, accident, old age, and death.

In the agricultural society, where several generations could live together as one family unit, subsistence did not depend exclusively upon the work of one man. The death or disability of the head of the family might temporarily cripple the enterprise but would not destroy it as a self-supporting unit. With urbanization, the economic security of the individual declined. The former simple arrangements that had operated to provide care for the disabled person and his family were no longer adequate in the complicated and industrialized society. In this new situation, man's age-old desire for security demanded the development of social and economic

19

mechanisms to meet the new needs. The growth of labor unions, the activities of liberal political groups, and the general awakening of a "social conscience" all contributed to the emergence of a new understanding of the rights and needs of the working man as an individual. Group life insurance was thus born in response to human needs born of the industrial age. "Group life" was founded on the principle of employer-employee cooperation to satisfy the requirements of the working man for security. This historical step initiated a movement of far-reaching social and economic significance in the United States.

Group Life. Group insurance had a modest beginning. The first group life policy was issued in 1911 by the Equitable to cover 121 employees of the Pantasote Leather Company of Passaic, New Jersey. In the next few years, a number of similar policies were issued by several insurance companies. Fifty-five years later, the number of contracts had grown to 233,000; and the volume of group life insurance in force in the United States was $306 billion, 34 percent of the principal amount of all life insurance then outstanding. This impressive growth reflects in part the rapid expansion of American industry in general; but perhaps more importantly, it reflects changes in our social institutions, in underlying social values, and in related human needs.

Although group life insurance was initially designed to provide modest protection to the family during the days of readjustment following the death of the breadwinner, another pressing problem of the industrial worker was the need for protection of his paycheck against the hazards of illness and injury.

Group Health. In 1915, some life insurance companies began to devise experiments to fill these needs, and by 1919 group disability income insurance was being widely written. The most recent growth of group insurance has been in the field of hospitalization and surgical and medical care. The first group hospital expense policy was issued as early as 1934; group surgical expense followed in 1938; and in that same year both forms of coverage were written to protect the dependents of employees.

"Major medical" expense coverage was intro-

21

duced in 1943 to complete the package of basic hospital, surgical, and medical care benefits.

Immediately after World War II, the Supreme Court held, in the famous Inland Steel decision, that pensions and other employee fringe benefits are subject to the collective bargaining process. This brought organized labor fully into the group insurance picture.

Major medical insurance has provided the most recent impetus to growth of group health insurance. Designed to take the brunt of catastrophic hospital, surgical, and medical expenses, it operates as a supplement to basic plans of coverage. Many variations of this basic concept have been developed and are in widespread use today. Group dental insurance, introduced in the early 1960s, is the most recent addition to the field of health insurance.

Thus, in a period of a little more than twenty years, health coverages were vastly expanded in response to pressures, new needs, and the incentives generated by a changing and developing society. Insurance companies now provide hospital protection benefits to more than 100 million people, with nearly half that number covered under major medical policies.

Pension Plans. The economic hazards of death, illness, or injury for the individual worker and his family were, as we have shown, ameliorated considerably by the creation and growth of group life and health insurance. The economic, social, and psychological implications of the need for security in old age present complex and additional problems. The individual's frequent inability to save enough to provide for old age places the burden for support on his children. Yet it seems clear that recent and current changes in family arrangements make it increasingly difficult for one generation to take on the support of another. The problem has been further aggravated in that the proportion of individuals over sixty-five years of age in the population has been increasing since the turn of the century. In 1900, 4 percent of the population were sixty-five or over; by 1975, it will be over 10 percent.

Long before the passage of the Social Security legislation, a number of employers had recognized the need for pensions for the older workers in industry and had attempted to make some provision

23

for them. Informal plans were established in many companies, but these were generally unsatisfactory because they were operated on a pay-as-you-go basis and pension reserves were rarely set aside. The employee had no assurance as to what he could expect at retirement or whether the payments, once begun, would continue. As industries grew larger, it became increasingly difficult for the employer to deal with the older employees on an individual basis. Consequently, the life insurance companies began to provide old-age protection for employees on an actuarially sound, contractual basis by applying the group principle to the purchase of annuities. Insured pension plans actually began to go into effect in the early 1920s, but it was not until later that insurance companies wrote contracts on an industry-wide basis.

Private pension plans today cover over 30 million persons, and this coverage is expected to be greatly expanded in the future. Management in general has come to recognize that financial security for pensioners is a proper charge on industry and that fair plans can be adopted without serious financial drain. There is, I believe, no essential conflict between the government pension plan (Social Security) and private programs. The one guarantees a broad-based floor of protection for most members of our society; the other builds upon that floor.

COLLECTIVE PROGRAMS AND SOCIAL VALUES

If group insurance can be thought of as an economic development designed to meet human needs in a rapidly changing society, so, too, must we describe such public programs as Social Security and Medicare. The historical fact that group insurance was invented some twenty-five years before the passage of the Social Security Act is some evidence of the readiness with which business enterprise has historically attempted to meet the challenge of change. The coexistence of government and private pension plans tends, however, to aggravate a growing concern that the values of thrift may be in jeopardy. Stated another way, the question is being asked: do collective systems for generating some measure of security—irrespective of whether they

25

are public or private—have the consequence of corroding and undermining individual responsibility?

Obviously there is no simple answer to such a question, but I am advised that some recent research on the matter is relevant and to a degree encouraging. The evidence from this research strongly suggests that the various automatic security providing programs are not tending to decrease additional savings—if anything, they are increasing them.

To my mind, the most powerful theory to explain such a result, if indeed, the findings ultimately bear it out, can be stated in terms of new motivation to attain goals that now appear realizable. If people see that intermediate savings goals are attainable, their inducements to continue to longer-range goals are greatly enhanced.

The point to emphasize here, however, is that a question such as this must be of great national concern. It carries important and immediate implications for the life insurance business, since it asks whether a higher or a lower proportion of the families currently participating in private pension plans

buy and own more life insurance than nonpartici-
pants.

Earlier in this discussion, different types of insurance coverage have been described which have
been innovated to meet changing human needs.
Let us now reverse the order and discuss the problems of social change which, in turn, are giving,
and will continue to give, rise to still different
modes of insurance protection. Let us, therefore,
focus attention upon the family and its probable
future.

The Family and Its Future

Many observers argue that the family as a social
institution is in the process of disintegration. Their
case goes something like this. Whereas the family
during the pre-industrial and pre-urbanized phases
in our society performed a wide variety of functions—economic, religious, political, recreational,
and educational—these functions have gradually
been taken out of the home and entrusted to more
efficient and more specialized social institutions.
Thus, the family today does little or no food processing; the family does relatively little educating

in any formal sense; the family today "officially" sponsors few religious activities. These functions are all now performed outside the home and the result, according to some, has been disastrous for the family. The family is now often viewed as being composed of members with highly individualistic and differing motivations, thus relegating the family group itself to instability. These social critics go on to cite divorce rates and juvenile delinquency statistics as if they also constituted evidence sealing the doom of the family.

Now this is no occasion to examine such a large sociological issue in depth; but let me offer an alternative interpretation which, in my opinion, gives a far better clue to what the future will be like. First and foremost, there is no sign that marriage and family are becoming unpopular in our culture. Indeed, the proportion of adults who are married and currently living with their spouses is at an all-time high in our history. This is a very impressive statistic. It comes at a time when it is very easy for a single woman to be independent and to support herself. It also comes at a time when there has been apparently a general relaxation of sex taboos.

of various kinds. If the family were on the way out, we would be justified in expecting to find a decline in the importance of the concept of home. But what are the facts? Since World War II, there has been an unprecedented boom in housing and the single-family dwelling has been in the highest demand. These are compelling considerations, especially now when the population is more mobile both geographically and occupationally than ever before.

Such evidence suggests that we may expect continued increase in the popularity of marriage. (At present rates, over 90 percent of both males and females will marry at some time in their lives.) The age of marriage may decline slightly in the future from current levels: an average of twenty for females and nearly twenty-three for males. We may also expect a continuation of the current tendency for increasing proportions of women to bear children, even though the birthrate may decline. We may also expect a continuation of the existing tendency to concentrate childbearing in the early years of marriage. By age thirty-five, the average mother is today sending her youngest child to school and so becomes available for at least limited membership in the labor force. Statistics show that in 1900 only one family in twenty had a working wife; today the figure is one in three. This trend is by no means confined to wives who work out of economic necessity. Women work at all income levels, and the tendency to work actually increases with the level of education. This, incidentally, is a social change of profound importance. Indeed, I suspect that there are few, if any, business enterprises today which are not faced, either directly or indirectly, with problems or opportunities created by this fundamental change in the American family. Certainly, for the life insurance business, it is of stunning significance.

These trends in family life also suggest that the traditional sharp division of masculine and feminine family roles is becoming blurred. Women are turning to occupational careers in increasing numbers; husbands are helping out with household tasks and are playing an increasingly important role in child rearing. Husbands and wives are making more decisions jointly. What this seems to mean is that the family will become increasingly specialized in performing its central function—that of bringing up the young and looking after the social, material, and emotional needs of its members.

Closely related to these considerations is a final point which deserves separate notice. The deliberate acceptance of financial responsibility lies behind the whole process of family formation. Our young adults remain oriented to the idea and ideals of family life and are apparently quite ready to take on the requisite responsibilities which go with the decision to marry and form a family. Perhaps never before have we seen such a responsible new generation of young householders.

While no one expects the family of the twenty-first century to be precisely like its twentieth century counterpart, current and anticipated changes carry with them no likelihood that the family will be replaced.

Many of the innovations adopted by life insurance companies in respect to the form and substance of policies are responsive to the needs of family members. A research study, for example, has pointed out that a substantial proportion of all individual life insurance policies are currently purchased through the so-called family plan policy or are included in policies with family plan riders. This type of family plan is of relatively recent origin. Furthermore, large amounts of new insurance coverage are produced under guaranteed insurability plans, an innovation which, like the family plan policy, was introduced to the American public by the life insurance business in recent years. The future, it is confidently believed, will see changes of far greater magnitude.

Public and Private Programs—Some Emerging Issues

So, too, will there be future changes in public programs for collective security; and here again, we shall be faced with decisions of great importance. It is the clear responsibility of the management of any business enterprise to conduct its affairs realistically and creatively in the context of the larger society of which it is a part. To be sure, responsible managers sometimes have proceeded to combat government on the basis of the simple argument that government activity should be restricted to the fullest possible extent. But life is not that simple. Even the most vocal exponents of this view know full well that our society could not survive in a world of change without the laws, rules, provisions, programs, and orderly processes of government. The range of responsibilities which must be assumed by government is enormous—from conservation to fair trade, from sanitation standards to fiscal policy, from the protection of free speech to the necessary exercise of police power. Moreover, there will be an increasing need for government and business to find bases for cooperative activity and a continuing and constructive partnership.

Several years ago, at an annual meeting of the Life Insurance Association of America, Mr. Devereux C. Josephs, the former chairman of the board of the New York Life Insurance Company, spoke eloquently and effectively on this matter. Mr. Josephs, who is in my judgment a wise and realistic man, has given me permission to use excerpts from this speech. He said, among other things:

> In my opinion, we should admit that the government, in one way or another, will have more and more influence upon our affairs: business, social, and educational. It follows, therefore, that

33

we should spend more of our time seeing how we can work with the government instead of against it. We will need to participate more in government and join with it in mapping our courses of future action. We had better concede that government, in spite of all its rules and regulations, is unavoidably our partner and not our traditional opponent.

My purpose is not to discuss the details of a proper division of activities between government and private enterprise in providing security programs. Nor do I propose to do more than illustrate the kind of partnership that may evolve. Rather, I would like to suggest two convictions that almost inevitably will become involved in future debate on related issues.

First, it is submitted that the division of activities should be guided by the philosophy that our public programs are operated to provide floors of protection, whereas our private programs are designed to enable individuals and groups to provide for themselves at levels of their own choosing and capacity. Obviously, these "floors" will have to change as conditions change; but the important element in the implementation of the theory is that the public programs are financed by payroll taxes imposed upon employers and employees, whereas the financing arrangements for private programs can vary enormously and freely, depending upon the particular requirements and means of the participants in any one program.

The second conviction is closely related and calls attention to the importance of capital formation in any constructive partnership. Although it is planned to discuss this matter in some detail in the second lecture in this series, it should be noted in passing that our nation cannot begin to employ the growing number of workers under a system of private enterprise unless the instruments for assembling pools of private savings—such as the life insurance companies, the savings institutions, and the investment banks—are able to go about this vital business. A pay-as-you-go tax simply cannot fill this bill. As we shall subsequently point out, this accumulation of private capital is not an end in itself—it is rather required, in the case of life insurance, as a reserve to guarantee future commitments; but it is nonetheless a basic product of the kind of enterprise under discussion.

35

In sum, the major part of a life insurance company's assets represents funds needed to make good on its promises to pay out money to its policyholders in the future. Meantime, these assets comprise present investments which essentially contribute to the economic well-being and future growth of the United States. But the problems are mighty and many. We shall consider this part of the story in a discussion entitled, "On the Use of Capital."

2

ON THE USE OF CAPITAL

INTRODUCTION

We have already noted that life insurance companies provide services not only to individuals but
to society as a whole. Through the process of providing a measure of indemnity for the value of
terminated lives, of writing annuities to sustain per-
sistent lives, and of furnishing other services of in-
demnification, they have accumulated, in virtual
trust for their policyholders, billions of dollars in
capital funds.

The ways in which these funds are employed
through investments are of significance in the first
instance to the policyholders, who are dependent
upon the safety and profitability of the assets held
for them. Such investments are of significance, in
the second instance, to the public generally, since
it must be our purpose as responsible investment
managers to see to it that the funds are used creatively and imaginatively to bring about ever-
increasing productivity and efficiency in such vital
areas as the facilities of production, both large

and small, downtown urban rebuilding, the means of transportation, the exploitation of the basic sources of energy, and the national supply of housing—to mention but a few.

The social and economic needs and problems of our time, however, are staggering and sometimes appear to be overwhelming. We can do no less than prepare ourselves to be responsive. Our investment policies provide a helpful vehicle in this regard.

Relevance of the Three Principles

This lecture, then, will discuss the investment function as it, in turn, operates to meet both individual and social needs in a fast-changing society. The story of this side of the life insurance business is essentially a story of past decisions, but perhaps more importantly, it reflects our eagerness to reach into the future. We are determined to be philosophically equipped, so far as may be, to meet the requirements of the foreseeable future—a task of greater potential value than the exhaustive exploitation of the present.

As we have emphasized earlier, the welfare of

the policyholder must receive first priority in any hierarchy of objectives involved in an investment decision. We have a commitment to him. Closely related to this, of course, is the necessity for the decisions to be such as to keep the company eminently sound and competitive. Of paramount importance, however, is the necessity of considering the far-flung and long-term social and economic consequences of the actual investment decisions.

INVESTMENT REQUIREMENTS

As a generator of savings, the character of life insurance differs fundamentally from that of deposit-type institutions in at least three important respects: (1) it is contractually long-term in nature; (2) it is motivated primarily by the desire for family or personal financial protection over extended periods of time; and (3) it is expected to be left intact until the contingency insured against arises, rather than withdrawn for current use. It is this set of characteristics which requires the life insurance companies to take explicit account of both near-term and long-term considerations in their operations. It also provides us with promising opportunities for seeking out new and imaginative ways of responding to the financial demands of our changing society. Consequently, the two traditional insurance investment criteria—safety and yield—should be assumed and thus may be dealt with briefly. It is the social content of our decisions that will command our primary attention.

The Safety Requirement

The very nature of the life insurance contract and the resulting liability to the policyholder dictate the adoption of investment policies that assure the safety of invested funds. The promise and the ability of the life company to meet promptly and in full all claims for benefits as they arise is the very essence of the insurance contract. At the same time, however, it would be incorrect to assume that life companies are unwilling to take reasonable investment risks. On the contrary, such risk taking must be part of our very philosophy as managers of these funds.

The Yield Requirement

In addition to the contractual feature of the "promise to pay," life insurance and annuity contracts are typically written and priced on the basis of an assumed rate of interest to be earned. In order to produce the requisite earnings, there inescapably exists a keen incentive to maximize the aggregate yield on the portfolio.

To the extent that life insurance companies are able to produce a higher net yield (after expenses, depreciation, and taxes) than that assumed, they are able to reduce the net cost of insurance through the dividend mechanism. Therefore, any particular company which can produce a comparatively higher net yield on its investments is in a more favorable cost position vis-à-vis its competitors.

RISK AND SAFETY—A GENERAL PROBLEM

It is suspected that the basic problem of reconciling the desire for the returns incident to risk with the need for safety is a familiar anxiety which daily confronts responsible American businessmen everywhere. Whatever may be the wide dimensions of our dilemma, we must recognize as basic criteria in the investment of policyholder reserves: (1) the consideration of principal safety, which is indispensable to the capacity to honor claims and (2) the strong incentive to maximize yield in order not only to meet contractual requirements but also to influence favorably, in the area of competition, the net cost of insurance.

THE PUBLIC INTEREST

In addition, and more importantly for our purposes here, the life companies view their investments as being in the nature of a public trust that should be scrupulously handled in the public interest. Although the rights and obligations of the parties arise from a contract and not from a trust, a social philosophy must permeate investment administration. There are, of course, times when a proposed investment may be fully eligible on grounds of safety and yield but has such dubious social values as to invite strong reservations. The case of gambling casinos is a good illustration. In such instances, the life companies typically have refrained from financing such undertakings. The lines, however, are far from clear, and they are constantly changing. The distinction between a pari-mutuel racetrack, a baseball park, bingo, the legalized slot machine, and a lottery is not an obvious one.

43

Monitoring the Future

But it is the positive rather than the negative which we would emphasize. The social, moral and economic problems of our society are bound to become more rather than less complex. Similarly, the investment opportunities which are constantly unfolding challenge us to be responsive to the new requirements of an increasingly technological society. It is necessary to take a long, hard look into the future. The rate of obsolescence is staggering. We must forecast whether our investments made today will be serving society's needs tomorrow in constructive and dynamic ways.

THE MOBILITY OF FUNDS AND CHANGING NEEDS

Let us turn, then, to a brief review of the role of life company funds in attempting to meet the changing needs of society.

Some Historical Examples

A quick look at the historical development of some of the major types of investments may be helpful. Consider, first, the railroads.

The Railroads. It is a fact of economic history that the expansion of the railroad system in this country was one of the most significant factors in the growth of the United States. Life insurance funds, however, played very little part in the early financing of the railroads. In 1870, for example, railroad securities represented only about 1 percent of the total assets of all the life companies. In retrospect, here was an investment opportunity which was clearly missed. But as the transcontinental and Western trunk lines developed and our transportation system spread throughout the land with mounting needs for heavy capital investment, the life insurance companies responded and provided vast funds. Railroad bonds reached their peak as a percentage of life insurance assets in 1906, when they represented more than one-third of the companies' aggregate invested reserves. At that time, Henry Clay Frick is reported to have remarked, "Railroads are the Rembrandts of investment." Since then, as we all know, railroad bonds have declined in every year as a percentage of insurance assets until they now amount to less than 2 percent.

The Utilities. Or consider the utilities. After

45

World War I came the great expansion of the electric utility and telephone industries. From a level of approximately 2 percent of assets in 1920, utility bond holdings of life insurance companies rose steeply until by 1937 they had become the largest class of life insurance bond investments. By 1940, public utility bond investments of the life insurance industry amounted to some 14 percent of all assets.

The Two World Wars. As we look back in these broad sweeps of recent history, another interesting illustration of the relationship of investments to social change arose in U.S. Treasury obligations used as part of the financing of this country's efforts in World War I. At the outbreak of hostilities abroad in 1914, the total amount of life insurance company holdings of government bonds was less than $1 million out of total assets of over $5 billion. But, during the war, the life companies invested almost their entire increase in assets in Treasury securities with the result that by 1919 such investments accounted for nearly 12 percent of total assets.

In the first half of the 1940s, the trend toward

U.S. government bonds began a new chapter as history repeated itself. During World War II, the insurance companies invested large sums in Treasury issues—more, in fact, than their net increase in assets during this same period. At the end of the war, these bonds totaled more than $20 billion in the combined portfolios of all life companies and constituted an unprecedented 46 percent of assets.

Mortgages and Real Estate. A similar pattern of capital responsiveness can be traced for different types of mortgages. Briefly, we might note the upsurge in farm mortgage loans beginning with the outbreak of World War I and continuing into the early 1920s as the United States, for the first time, assumed the role of "bread basket of the world." By 1921, farm mortgages represented nearly 18 percent of life company assets, a greater share than that of all other mortgages. With a return to world peace and more traditional food marketing patterns, however, the need for farm mortgage financing diminished and this type of asset decreased in importance.

But as farm mortgages declined, urban mortgages expanded rapidly in reflection of the building boom of the 1920s and the accompanying need for long-term financing. By 1930, urban mortgages accounted for some 30 percent of all life insurance company assets. With the subsequent stagnation of the economy and the government demands for defense funds from 1940 through 1945, urban mortgage debt declined in relative importance.

With the great housing boom which followed World War II, the life companies again directed their reserve assets into this area of financial need. Initially, the surge of funds went into one-to-four-family residences as the nation sought to provide adequate housing and as social values became more strongly committed than ever before to individual home ownership.

Later, the flow of mortgage funds emphasized industrial and commercial properties, as shopping centers emerged to serve a growing suburban population and as office buildings dominated urban construction to accommodate industrial and business growth as well as the shift from blue-collar to white-collar employment.

Most recently, apartment house financing has become an important user of life insurance funds as the forces of the real estate marketplace reflect and anticipate the vast housing needs arising out of the wave of new marriages and family formations by the generations born during and after World War II and now entering adulthood. Thus, in the mortgage area, as in the securities area, life insurance funds have been highly mobile both in responding to and, to some extent, in anticipating the needs of a rapidly growing and changing society—sometimes at war, sometimes at peace.

We are, however, far from satisfied with the record. The problems are great—particularly those which inhere in our so-called metropolitan areas—and to a consideration of these, we shall return.

Some Recent Developments

In this regard, important attention must be given to the current climate of innovation and technological change.

Innovation. There is, for example, the interesting development of the taconite mill in the production of iron. In the Mesabi Range, as you will recall, vast quantities of taconite and low-grade ore were being left in the ground. It was discovered,

49

however, that in all probability, it would be economically feasible to crush the taconite, extract the iron ore by a magnet, and roll it into pellets to be used in making steel. A contract with the mines was subsequently proposed to supply the taconite, and another agreement was made with the mills to produce the pellets for sale to the steel industry. Under this unprecedented arrangement, a group of life companies committed millions of dollars to finance the first taconite pellet plant at Silver Bay, Minnesota. Other taconite mills followed in other iron mining areas; employment and income recovered. Not only was a region saved from stagnation but an unused basic resource had been put to work.

The life insurance companies also anticipated the future as reflected in the long-term debt financing of the first private atomic power plant, the facility at Rowe, Massachusetts, operated by the Yankee Atomic Electric Company. A generation ago it would have been impossible to imagine an insurance company investing large sums of money in an atomic power plant.

The financing of the acquisition of jet planes by

private airlines was another innovation in which the insurance industry played an important role. C. R. Smith, chairman of American Airlines, has recently observed that:

> Credit for the jet revolution should go to the three principal participants: the manufacturers, . . . the airlines, . . . and the financial institutions, with faith in the enterprise and willingness to provide the long-term credits needed to finance the project.
>
> A high percentage of the long-term loans came from the insurance companies and they should have credit for their major part in bringing about the jet revolution.

Post-war Growth. Finally, perhaps the broadest response to the changing needs of American society has been the flow of insurance funds into industrial bonds in the post-World War II years, an era of unprecedented economic growth. Until the 1930s, life insurance companies had virtually no investments in industrial bonds, and even as late as 1945, this class of investment represented less than 5 percent of all assets. Since that time, industrial obligations have grown to be the most favored class of bonds in the life insurance companies, with the result that their holdings had grown, at the close of 1966, to some 25 percent of total assets.

THE THREE PRINCIPLES IN REVIEW

The foregoing account, upon which we most certainly cannot rest our case for the future, leads me to restate the three guiding principles with which we began. The most immediate responsibility of any life company in its investment operations is to be a trusted and responsible steward for the individual policyholders. Closely related, of course, is the responsibility of the company for its own efficient operations—its competitive position in terms of rate of return vis-à-vis other companies of comparable size and character.

In addition, the life companies, to a degree, at least, have seized opportunities to initiate and participate in investment programs that support the imaginative entrepreneur and that foster economic growth and advance the standard of living. This, then, is our third and most profound responsibility. We must serve in the future far more effectively and in a wider area as trustees of large pools of private savings to the end that they may be made boldly available for long-term investment for the capital requirements and ever-expanding needs of our entire society.

SOME EMERGING PROBLEMS

In these social respects, however, we are not without gnawing problems. I would discuss two of these with you: the need for capital formation and the need for community development.

In the first place, we are desperately concerned about the nation's vital needs for future capital formation.

The Need for Capital Formation

Of one thing we can be sure, we will be faced over the next decade with a huge demand for capital funds. We are today on the threshold of an enormous increase in our labor force, and we are simultaneously the world's first trillion-dollar economy of a single nation. In 1975, our labor force will exceed 93 million persons, an increase of 15 million over the 1965 figure. The number one challenge before us is to provide the jobs needed to employ this surging tide of manpower.

53

To attain this employment objective will require a huge increase in private investment, and this, in turn, is dependent upon capital formation. In one of its research studies, the National Industrial Conference Board estimates that by 1975 nonresidential fixed investment needs will require an annual expenditure of over $118 billion. This estimate indicates a need for growth in the annual rate of capital investment during the period from 1964 to 1975, 15 percent higher than the expected growth during the same period in total gross national product. This means there must be jobs available which, in turn, means we must have the economic growth which can only come about if there is adequate capital to finance the new and expanded plants and facilities so badly needed.

To form such huge quantities of capital, an important role must be accorded to the accumulation of private savings. Professor Simon Kuznets of Harvard in his monumental study entitled "Capital in the American Economy: Its Formation and Financing," warns: "The demand for capital over the coming two and a half to three decades is likely to be large. . . . Under the circumstances, the supply of voluntary savings may not be adequate."

The life insurance industry, together with all other mechanisms for encouraging saving, must, it seems to me, take all possible steps to help to meet the rising need for capital funds. We should, consequently, foster close coordination and integration with Federal programs and measures to the end that we are not impaired in our ability to accumulate capital. Some recent developments in Canada and Europe bear on this problem. The experience in Canada is revealing and possibly prophetic. Following the promulgation of the recent Canadian and Quebec Government Pension Plans, there arose not only a negative effect on the installation of new private pension programs but, because of pension plan "cash ins," a significantly reduced flow of funds available for investment by Canadian life insurance companies.

Our European friends are also concerned with the need to accumulate savings to promote long-term investment and economic growth. An important conference on capital markets was recently sponsored by the Atlantic Institute and the Business and Industry Advisory Council of the Organization for Economic Cooperation and Development. It was there concluded that sound economic growth requires strengthened and improved capital markets. It was further agreed that the capital markets of Continental Europe must be stimulated by cooperative action between government, industry, and financial institutions and that one of the primary policy objectives of government should be to encourage contractual savings institutions like life insurance companies and pension funds. The United States was held up as the model of a desirable capital market which accumulates savings for long-term investment from private sources and not from government, as is the case in Continental Europe.

The Need for Community Development

Let us turn now to a second and even more pervasive problem—the need for community development. We live in a period of transition to an ever-expanding metropolitan *society* rather than in well-established and defined metropolitan *communities*. Indeed, one doesn't have to look far to find commentators, who quite seriously raise the question as to whether man can develop an adequate sense of community within the impersonal, anonymous, and confusing conditions of our vast metropolitan areas. Urban sprawl, downtown blight, to say nothing of a wide range of social problems—crime, divorce, alcoholism, juvenile delinquency, drug addiction, graft and corruption—are all cited as evidences of past failures. The number and complexity of such problems will predictably increase during the next two decades. For any type of business enterprise primarily concerned with people, such as life insurance, to stand aloof from this agonizing predicament is not only unthinkable but, in fact, impossible. To be sure, we are directly or indirectly involved in many specific programs having to do with equal employment opportunity, rehabilitation procedures, corporate citizenship, comprehensive medical care, and continuing education. But we tend, I fear, to look upon these as crash programs rather than as long-term commitments. David Rockefeller recently said of New York City, "The most important thing the big companies here can do is to stay in the city and do an efficient, profitable job." This is, of course, a basic necessity. But

57

we should and can do more—perhaps much more.

At least three major social upheavals are now in process which illuminate the severity of the problems and underscore the need for new approaches to community development.

Demographic Changes. The first of these is a demographic change, especially the striking change in the age composition of the population. Babies born during the peak birthrate years just after World War II are now reaching young adulthood. Predictably, the rate of new household formation will soon hit a new high. At the other end of the age scale, the demographic revolution is producing some equally important changes. Not only will there be a dramatic increase in the population aged sixty-five and over, but it is quite clear that these older people will continue to maintain separate and independent households. Both of these circumstances call for new and appropriately designed, priced, and financed housing, expanded educational and training facilities, more job opportunities, and more cultural and recreational resources.

Changes in the Labor Force. The second major upheaval is the radical shift in the nature of the labor force now required because of advancing technology. This is a shift both in the numbers of workers required and in the kinds of occupations for which they must be carefully recruited and technically trained. Increasingly specialized educational programs will be required.

Social and Economic Discrimination. The third force now acting persistently and painfully upon our cities is the heightened awareness among both minority and majority groups of the still existing social and economic discrimination which conflicts with basic American democratic principles. This is, in part, due to the fact that modern technology, at least for the time being, has actually wiped out more and more of the lower-level jobs which once served as initial opportunities for entrants to the labor force.

Thus we have coexisting these great social phenomena—demographic change, new labor force requirements, and racial discrimination—all interacting to aggravate urban problems.

The fact is that a great deal of effort—to say nothing of funds—has been devoted to large-scale urban redevelopment for more than a decade; but

59

the results, at least in human terms, have been disappointing. In the light of this experience, it is our job in business to seek out the reasons why our efforts have not been more successful and to take remedial action.

Factors Impeding the Solution of Urban Problems

There are, I submit, at least two considerations which provide some light on our failure to have greater success in these matters. The first is the frequent tendency to forget that human beings are motivated by appetites, problems, and dreams. A second condition which hinders our urban redevelopment efforts is the increasing political and social complexity of our metropolitan areas.

Failure to Consider Human Values. In the last analysis, cities are people. Thus a fundamental reason for some of our disappointments may have been the failure to give sufficient thought to the real needs of the people who were actually to be affected by the proposed renewal programs. Low-cost housing projects seem to be a good illustration. It was widely believed that decent, cheap housing would enable the debt- and problem-ridden slum dwellers to get back on their feet, restore their health and morale as well as their solvency, and eventually enable them to move up in their social and economic scale and possibly out of the area. We know now, of course, that it is not enough to change the physical environment—a whole way of life is involved. There exists a slum culture, which cannot just be wished away or left behind.

Furthermore, social scientists tell us that any remedial program—such as a housing reform—has a very poor chance of successfully meeting human needs if the people affected resist the change. Our community development programs might well encourage greater participation and enlist the voluntary help of the informal but tight groupings which are to be found in the local social organizations of city neighborhoods.

Complexity of the Metropolis. Turning to the second factor which impedes community development, it seems clear that constructive urban design must be both planned and implemented within the context—not of separate cities—but of vast and ever-expanding metropolitan areas.

61

Transportation provides an excellent illustration of a set of problems which must be met on a wide metropolitan basis, in a way that transcends local loyalties and jurisdictions.

The problem of our cities, in short, is a complex of many interlocking and overlapping problems—transportation, housing, education, local cultures, population change, and countless others. Each of these problems, quite understandably, has its own corps of specialists, but herein may lie the basic difficulty. Most of us become specialists in one field or another, and we tend to talk and associate only with other specialists in the same field. There is nothing more frustrating than to observe a group of specialists struggling to find the solution to a general problem.

The Need for an Integrated Effort

As a businessman who has seen the management team operate with reasonable success under a variety of conditions, it makes sense to me to learn more about the great variety of team systems and interdisciplinary approaches to long-range urban design and community development.

There are many models to choose from, one of which is an approach to urban problems which, appropriately enough, has its home in Athens—an approach with which I am sure many of you are familiar. This is known as "ekistics"—taking its name from the Greek word for home. It calls for the closest possible collaboration between the technical and cultural disciplines—engineering and architecture—on the one hand, and the behavioral sciences and public administration, on the other. If such a science is ever to be evolved and applied, public and private interests must walk hand in hand.

At a recent annual symposium, which traditionally holds its last session on the ancient island of Delos, this international group specified the purpose of this new discipline to "bring together separate approaches . . . and fragmented facets of policy . . . and set them to work together on the new problems . . . of man in his dynamic and increasingly urban environment."

We can do no less than to wish such groups well in their endeavors. It is my firm conviction that man is intelligent enough to undo the confusion which he has created. If our social problems are great, so are our talents, our resources, and our determinations.

CONCLUDING NOTE

I have, however, no clear-cut answers or ready solutions to offer. Rather, I would conclude this discussion simply by reemphasizing our awareness of these problems and restating the spirit in which we approach them.

Certainly, there is much to be done both by public leaders and private managers in enhancing still further both the quality and the level of the American standard of life. But these programs call for widening rather than limiting the areas of public and private cooperative effort. This is especially applicable in the investment field, where private funds have served, along with tax dollars, to contribute to the development of community life. The life insurance companies have for over 100 years attempted to serve the public interest and the needs of our society in this regard.

But, as I have suggested, the problems have become increasingly severe and, for my part, I believe that we, in the life insurance industry, should engage in searching, dynamic, bold, and imaginative schemes directed toward their solution. I believe that we should espouse programs which will encourage us to invest more, to be even more experimental, and to take more rather than fewer risks in the future of metropolitan America. Perhaps we need a new concept of venture capital in the social field. I do not pretend to be wise enough to know. But in the meantime, I believe that we, of the industry, can pledge our best efforts to the end that we may continue to fulfill our historic role in helping to meet the vital capital needs of the future.

3

ON SERVING SOCIAL CHANGE

INTRODUCTION

As businessmen, our responsibility in serving social change is great. Our responsibility to serve it well is even greater. It seems appropriate, therefore, on this occasion to discuss some of our basic concerns, hopes, and plans for the future and for the American society, as a whole, to which we are all so deeply committed and in which we have such large stakes.

The Three Principles Illustrated

In the first lecture of this series, we mentioned certain important ways in which man's security needs are met by life insurance and annuity contracts. Then, in the second lecture, we took note of the investment function and some of the vital social consequences which can and do flow from it. Throughout these discussions we have underscored three principles which we believe to be applicable to business in general: (1) to give priority to the advancement of individual human values and the

68

well-being of people; (2) to keep our enterprises growing in strength and service through innovation and response to change; and (3) to take the long view—to recognize ourselves as units in an interdependent whole and thus to relate our decisions to the welfare of the larger society in which we live. These three principles are not mutually exclusive. Their elements, as we have seen, are inextricably intertwined.

During this last lecture, we shall illustrate how the observance of these principles affects our reaction to the demands of the future.

The Problem of the Future

Although it is relatively easy to imagine and even predict such dramatic technological developments as supersonic travel, systems of communications satellites, underwater agriculture, electronic highways, or even computerized homes, it's much more difficult to anticipate and foretell their social consequences.

Let it be admitted at the outset, that we know very little about the controlling factors in any detail. We do know that more than a third of all of us alive today will not live to see the year 2000. (Some of us, indeed, may not want to.) Or, put another way, we know that of the total American population who will witness the turn of the century, three-quarters are yet to be born. It is probably reasonable, however, to suggest that although our society thirty-five years from now will be vastly different from what it is today, it will inevitably be rooted in both our past and present values.

What this means is that the social and economic changes between now and then will not be entirely haphazard. What we do today will in no small measure determine the kind of society which we will have when the nation enters the new century.

Certain controlling developments can be assumed with some degree of confidence: (1) Our understanding and our conquest of the physical universe will have been vastly extended. (It cannot be predicted that lunar weekends will be frequent, but apparently there will be men well established on the moon.) (2) Our knowledge of man both as a physiological and as a psychological organism will be far greater than it is today. (Recently Dr. René

Dubos disclosed some startling evidence that only between 5 and 10 percent of our genes are really at work—the great bulk are immobilized by the inhibitions of the environment. He feels sure that a higher percentage will become operative.) (3) Our knowledge of man's basic social institutions will be more profound. (As to this, we shall have more to say presently.) Many of these matters may be quite specifically predicted. The real question, however, lies not in the detail of differences which will take shape between now and the turn of the century. The real question is—will the world in its entirety be a better place for mankind?

Although we can't answer this big question with any precision, we must not overlook a profound and long-established fact of life. Unless we believe that the world will be a better place in the future, it may very well turn out not to be. Thus, even the dream of utopia may turn out to have great practical value. It is easy to be discouraged by the complexity of anticipating the future; but it is believed that if we work faithfully for a good future, the future will reflect our work. This is what the Columbia sociologist Robert Merton calls "a self-fulfilling prophesy."

We propose to discuss two types of change—each of which illustrates in quite different ways our underlying concerns. We return, first, to our earlier discussion of the family, paying special attention to changing human needs and our plans for serving them. In the second place, we shall recount the story of how, in our particular enterprise of life insurance, we have come to terms with the computer revolution. In effect, we shall ask what the future will be like in reference to these two basic dimensions of our changing society—patterns of family life and the new relationship of man to the machine.

THE CHANGING FAMILY CYCLE

Changes, important changes, are indubitably taking place in that most basic of all social institutions—the family. A new phase is being developed in the family cycle. There has evolved a greatly extended period of joint survival of husband and wife in the middle and later years. Such extension of years of joint survival foreshadows a new kind of family enterprise. Millions of American families are now, and in the future will be, caught up in trends which prophesy such an outcome. Let us examine some well-known and vital facts.

The Decline in Male Work-life Expectancy

Between 1900 and 1960, approximately eighteen years were added to male life expectancy at birth. These added years have been distributed about equally between an increase in work life and an increase in the years lived outside the labor force. The four or five years which have been added before embarking upon a work career create valued and unprecedented educational opportunities. The added retirement years disclose the significance of this lengthened period in the life cycle and especially expose the high potential value of the leisure time which is now available.

Recently, however, a remarkable event has taken place: man's work-life expectancy began to decline. Whereas his expected time outside the labor force has continued to rise, the prediction is that this new trend toward a shorter work life will be maintained, as the age of retirement continues to drop.

This means that a man's working life will be more and more compressed into his middle years, as the so-called "nonproductive" years are extended.

Earlier Retirement. The rate of participation in work by males sixty-five years and older has declined steadily over the past sixty or seventy years. In 1900, for example, nearly 70 percent of all older males were in the active labor force, in contrast with less than 30 percent today and probably no more than 25 percent by 1975. When this is related to the dramatic increase in the joint survival years, husbands and wives can look forward to an extended period of retirement which never before existed. In the light of this fact, it is hard to believe that just prior to the turn of this century there was less than a fifty-fifty chance that both parents would be alive at the time their youngest child was married.

Extended Education. The period of formal education continues to be extended with increasing proportions of students going on to college and professional and graduate schools. A decade ago, relatively few undergraduates went directly on to some kind of graduate study; but today the figure is constantly rising, and for some universities it now approaches three out of four. Nor are these young people delaying their marriages. They are studying and establishing new families at the same time.

Married Women in the Labor Force

The new life cycle of the family invites the participation of married women in the labor force. This is a relatively new historical phenomenon. In 1900, only one family in twenty had a working wife; in 1965, this was true of one in every three families.

Two phases in the working life of married women must be distinguished. Wives are most likely to work for brief periods before their first pregnancy and again, for longer periods of time, after their children are established in school or are on their own. Indeed, we seem to be approaching a period in American history when almost all wives will work at some time.

Male and Female Work Patterns—a Contrast

Although the work-life patterns of women are generally similar to those of men, there is at least one striking difference. Female life expectancy

75

since 1900 has increased more than twenty-two years. But the sharpest related gain has been in women's work life.

To make the contrast very clear—men are now spending fewer years of their lives *in* the labor force; women are spending fewer years of their lives *outside* the labor force.

There have arisen basic shifts in attitudes toward the working of women. Although many wives now work—especially the better-educated and high-status wives—it is interesting to recall that as recently as 1945, public opinion polls showed that the overwhelming majority of adult Americans expressed disapproval of wives becoming gainfully employed outside the home. The current attitude, which, of course, is largely positive, seems to reflect a shift in family values and customs which inescapably affects the relationship between husbands and wives. There is, for example, far less division of labor within the home and far more joint decision making as wives become increasingly sophisticated in regard to matters of business and finance.

Furthermore, there is a marked tendency for both the younger and older generations to maintain separate households. Thus, it is quite acceptable for young people to marry and form new households before becoming economically independent; but older people also are insisting upon independence and are typically reluctant to accept financial aid, even when it is offered by their married offspring.

The Problem—Income Maintenance over the Entire Cycle

In a word, as we enter the last third of the twentieth century, we are adding nonproductive years at both ends of the family cycle. Work is being compressed into the middle years, leaving to be supported longer periods both of youthful education and preparation and of post employment retirement. These changed circumstances raise important questions for business in general and life insurance in particular. One crucial question which is asked with increasing urgency is what are the available mechanisms for spreading out more evenly over the entire life cycle of the family the income which is earned during the middle years?

Although the family has various means available

for such leveling of income (for example, savings, insurance, private pension plans, etc.), serious and sizable problems remain: older people today are, relatively, still inadequately provided for; the costs of higher education for the young become ever more staggering; and a whole new set of demands is developing in regard to retirement. Consequently, some are urging that these problems should and will be solved not by the family but by complex and compulsory transfers of income via taxation for such specific purposes as expanded public education and extensions of Social Security.

Toward a Possible Solution—the Two-income Family

The emergence of the so-called "two-income" family may help to provide a different and to many a more acceptable solution. We do not yet fully understand the implications of this trend. But we do know this. Wives contribute substantially to the family's income. Indeed, at the $10,000 to $15,000 family income level, their contributions amount to almost a third of the total. We also know something of how this income is spent. For example, a recent survey of consumer finances showed that higher amounts were being expended on retirement plans by families in which there was a second income. Although more evidence is needed, there are several indications that the earnings of the wife are allocated to the higher education of their children (or their grandchildren) and to plans for retirement.

As social research further tests this hypothesis and continues to uncover in detail the changes that are taking place in the American family, many far-reaching implications for security needs will become apparent. Husbands and wives will inevitably seek new types of plans to meet such needs, all of which is a concern and an opportunity for the life insurance industry. New mechanisms for helping families spread their aggregate income over the entire life cycle must and will be developed, new needs must be met and new services offered, and new markets must be developed and new types of products sold.

The Life Insurance Salesman

In this last connection, these changes seem destined to pose new problems for the marketing and distribution of life insurance, since the meaning of security itself seems to be undergoing change. Man's quest for security has always raised, and probably will continue to raise, highly personal paradoxes since the most intimate aspects of life are inevitably involved: one's financial worth, one's innermost feelings about family relationships, one's adaptation to the fact that life is finite and that death is inevitable—even the definition of one's own identity and where and how one fits into the larger scheme of things. Since all of such matters are highly intimate and essentially threatening, we tend to submerge them. Certainly they are not subjects for casual conversation. Although we sometimes may joke about money, sex, and family relations, and even about death, these are the very considerations which must be brought into full and serious view when any form of security involving commitment is under consideration.

As the conditions of family life change, so will these hidden dimensions change. Greater and greater demands will be placed upon life insurance salesmen, indeed upon all types of financial advisers, to become increasingly sophisticated and sensitive to such changes. Perhaps some of these highly intimate considerations—previously largely repressed—will tend over time to become easier for the individual to explore on his own; but the probabilities are great that life insurance contracts, at least, will have to be sold by agents who must encourage their clients to think realistically about topics which continue to be both threatening and very personal. It is the rare man who, on his own, is able to initiate such considerations. Already the sales forces of the large life companies are being drastically overhauled. Most companies today insist upon well educated, fully committed, and dedicated men and women who can deal efficiently, and with great tact and dignity, with precisely the kinds of changes in American life which we have been discussing.

THE PROMISE OF AUTOMATION

We have been talking about income. Let us now turn to the work which produces it. For many generations, the purpose and significance of work has been closely related to personal human values which are of central importance to life insurance: we refer to thrift, responsibility, individual initiative, and the satisfaction of achievement. In recent times, however, a disturbing question has been raised. Under the impact of automation, is work losing its meaning as a driving human force? If there is any validity to this hypothesis, the life insurance industry, along with business in general will need to reexamine many of its basic assumptions.

On the other hand, this is not merely a philosophical question. As responsible businessmen we are trained to seek out and embrace any kind of innovation which enhances the efficiency of our enterprises or improves our competitive positions. The computer and its usefulness is the most familiar example.

The Computer—a Case Report

The early fears that man would be conquered by the machine have, of course, been dispelled by the facts. To be sure, automation has taken over many assembly-line jobs, but experience to date with the cybernetic revolution is that man is still very much in control. The big problem has to do with the speed of technological change.

A Recent Phenomenon. It is not quite fifteen years since the first time a meeting of life insurance people was held to discuss this subject. In late 1952, when that meeting took place, there were few in the life insurance business—or in any other business for that matter—who had ever given more than a passing thought to that new, strange phenomenon called the "electronic computer." As a matter of general interest, the newspaper accounts of the early machines interested most of us. That these machines might be increasingly useful to scientists, engineers, and research directors was not hard to imagine. But that they would become our own business tools, used day in and day out in our offices, not only in performing our routine functions but also in forward planning and decision making—such ideas, it is believed, were not then entertained by the great majority of life insurance executives.

In most types of business enterprise, office work supports the production line, and automation of office work is, in a sense, secondary to automation of the *factory*. In the life insurance business, automation of our office work *is* automation of the *factory*. Along with banks, public utilities, and other similar institutions, we have a particularly large stake in developments that make office work more efficient. And perhaps the special time perspective of our business (i.e., the servicing contracts that may be in effect over many decades) gives us an added impetus for measuring the importance of better data processing and recording procedures. Yet this may not be the main point of the story. Rather, it occurs to me that the major achievement to date has been an intangible one: the change from an attitude of experimentation to a conviction that the computer has now become an accepted part of our way of life. The feeling of experimentation—an attitude on the sidelines of "let's wait and see"—has been replaced by general familiarity, overall confidence, and large investments.

There have existed broad problems of policy that have faced the management of a life insurance company which was embarking on a full-scale electronics program. In particular, there were the "computer created" problems that went beyond the areas of technical specialization and performance. These problems dealt, for example, with personnel, organization, environmental change, etc. In pointing to some of these, I can only draw on our own company's experience; but many of the experiences involved must be quite general even though the details will vary according to different types of business.

Concern for Employees. In our adoption of electronic data-processing equipment, the number one problem had to do with the impact on individual employees. When manual operations are to be replaced by machine procedures, the result will be to reduce clerical jobs below the number that would otherwise be required. Under these circumstances, it is only natural that individual employees will be anxious about their own future. Our first step, consequently, was to see to it that this natural concern was recognized and allayed.

As I believe has been quite generally the case, we at the Equitable repeatedly assured all employees that no one would lose his or her job as the result of the electronics program. Normal turnover, particularly at the levels where the automation effect would be the greatest, accounted for many more resignations in a year than we could possibly match with specific jobs eliminated by automation. The growth of our business, both in volume and in depth, was continually opening up new jobs. The new electronics activity itself was already creating new opportunities in the fields of system design, programming, and machine operation. For these and other reasons, the problem of human displacement by the machine did not prove to be difficult.

In addition, we had to consider the specific job preferences and occupational experiences of each individual employee; we had to find a new place for each man or woman displaced in an area undergoing change. This was not always easy. Employees whose jobs were affected in one part of the company were not always the most suitable or best qualified for openings arising in another part. Normal turnover rarely matched exactly the timing and extent of job reduction resulting from automation. To this day, we have found no general foolproof solution to the problem: we have simply made sure that a responsible, understanding official takes charge of every case and keeps at it until an acceptable answer is found.

Organizational Consequences. We have had to recognize, too, that the introduction of the computer has had profound effects on the corporate structure of our organization. Since the early days, more than 100 years ago, we have divided our work into functional segments and created separate organizational units to correspond to these segments. It has been the right course, in the past, to departmentalize function-by-function—to have, say, one group of people responsible for billing and recording premium collections, another to deal with dividend work, and so on. But the computer has successfully challenged this theory. Electronic data-processing equipment gives the best overall results when related functions are integrated to the greatest possible degree.

Let me illustrate our approach to these new conditions. Our first electronics work was concentrated in the area of insurance administration, and in 1956 we changed our departmental organization to fit the new systems that were being developed. In our table of organization, a department is the major operating element. Consequently, we formed new departments, combining elements from several existing departments, in order to place under one head the various functions that were brought into new and close relationship with each other by the common usefulness of electronic data-processing.

In complex and particularly large organizations, there should be no such thing as isolation among departments. No matter what the alignment of functions on the charts and in the executive orders, every department with a basic operating responsibility will be dependent in one way or another on almost all, if not all, the company's other departments. Claims people need premium, dividend, loan, and other data to do their work. Field officers must operate under standard procedures designed to mesh directly with the operations of the home office. Policy records established as the result of underwriting and issue activities must fit into administrative operations and provide the field men with what they need.

It is ironic that the machine is forcing cooperation and an acceptance of mutual interdependence when man—though recognizing the evils of "little empires" and allegiance only to one's own specialty—has heretofore failed to adequately attain these goals.

Work procedures that cross departmental lines, consequently, should be built upon mutual understanding and confidence. It is consequently highly significant that it simply isn't possible to operate a system dependent upon electronic equipment without very close cooperation among those responsible for creating the original information, those who determine what is to be done with it, and those who use the end results. So far as I know, it remains one of the drawbacks of even the most advanced machine that it cannot—as humans can—adjust itself automatically to unexpected variations in the programming and interpretation of data.

More Demanding Jobs. Because our new and miraculous machines cannot adapt themselves automatically to even the smallest change from what they have been programmed to expect and deal with, we must—whenever we want to use them—learn to say *precisely* what we want them to do. This is not characteristic behavior for most of us:

89

we are more accustomed to saying *approximately* what we want, leaving it to those who are to carry out the work to fill in the gaps with normal imagination or, if they have to, to come back and ask questions when something unexpected develops. The requirement that we make the supreme effort to know exactly what we want in advance is, of course, what underlies the point made previously in speaking of the need for a greater degree of mutual understanding among those who share responsibility for a given area of work.

Problems and Opportunities

We have dealt at some length on the implications of the computer because it will inevitably continue to present us with new problems and opportunities. The United States recently became the first society in the history of the world in which less than half of its employed people are engaged in the production of tangible goods. Our greatest current manpower demands, consequently, are for men and women with special service "know-how" —that is those trained in the professional and technical occupations which require the most education. It now seems likely that the painful short-ages of human resources that we are experiencing today in the many fields which require extended training and a high level of competence will continue into the future.

Consequently, the future will call for broad preparation and the ability to absorb new knowledge and information throughout one's career. The worker of the future predictably will change his occupation—even his field of work—several times during his work life. He will need greatly expanded opportunities to acquire new skills. He will also need opportunities to become familiar with the social skills which will give him the adaptability and flexibility to move not only occupationally but also geographically and socially. Of one thing I think we can be quite sure: the worker of the future will favor the enterprise in which the work to be done has been organized in meaningful, rewarding, and purposeful ways.

Furthermore, we can be confident that the third and fourth generation of computers will play roles which today we can scarcely imagine—in forward planning; in managerial problem solving and decision making; in portfolio management; in creating models for the recruitment, selection, and development of manpower; and in unraveling the tangle of interlocking forces, needs, and pressures which characterize large and complex organizations.

Let us conclude this discussion with a recapitulation of some of the demands of the future.

THE DEMANDS OF THE FUTURE

The Institute of Life Insurance has recently called on its member companies to cooperate in a project entitled "The Future Outlook." As its name suggests, this project is designed to explore the dimensions of change as they may provide opportunities or create problems for our business. At a recent meeting of various task groups at the Arden House campus of Columbia University, Blake Newton, the president of the institute, aptly observed that "this business is inextricably caught up in the social and economic fabric of our time."

I believe that all businessmen would be moved to echo this sentiment. For quite apart from such pressing problems as urban renewal, suburban political boundaries, rapid transit, ethnic integration, educational resources, and regional planning, perhaps our central problem—as we approach the final third of the twentieth century—is how to capture the sense of community which has characterized our society until the relatively recent past. As we have repeatedly emphasized in these lectures, these tasks can only be made feasible through the joint and cooperative efforts of public and private groups. A defensive posture of business against government or an overriding policy of government against business are as out of date as the robber barons or "the big stick." The problems we face must be shared, and the dream of a better America will become a reality only through our joint and cooperative efforts.

The life insurance business, I submit, has specific commitments and obligations on these several fronts. In becoming increasingly sensitive and responsive to subtle changes in our basic social institutions, life insurance should be able to make a positive contribution to the sense of security which is basic to all forms of community life. As Dr. Davis Gregg, president of the American College of Life Underwriters, has recently written, ". . . the overriding question before us relates to . . . security for individuals and families in our society and the optimal methods of achieving it." Similarly, through its investment function, the industry is in a key position to contribute to the accumulation and flow of the funds needed in the constant revitalization and extensive rebuilding process which will be required during the final third of this century. The estimates vary, but it seems probable that by the turn of the century we shall have to have doubled our total metropolitan resources—productive and educational facilities, housing and transportation —to say nothing of a host of new needs as yet unspecified.

We are, then, far from satisfied with what we are doing in the here and now. As an industry, we face both problems and opportunities:

1. With respect to community redevelopment, it may well be that we should regularly allocate a percentage of our investable funds as a kind of venture capital—one, incidentally, which I suspect would pay handsome dividends.

2. With respect to income maintenance and pension plans, we must seek new ways to enhance benefits, to increase the portability of the individual

pension, and to make pensions more realistically responsive to the developing requirements of retirement and old age.

3. With respect to comprehensive health care, we must work with public and private groups at all levels to set even higher standards and to improve the delivery of health services (particularly the newly discovered procedures) to those who need them and yet keep the costs within bounds.

4. With respect to the distribution and marketing of insurance, we must continue to recruit, educate, and train our professional salesmen so that they can efficiently, intelligently, and with dignity provide their clients with the security programs which all people so understandably need and want.

5. With respect to our work environments, we must provide equal opportunities for all who would work with us; we must develop more challenging programs for young trainees and continuing education for all employees irrespective of status or level.

6. With respect to the threats of inflation, we must preserve the integrity of the life insurance contract yet, in ways still to be devised, see to it that our policyholders are not unnecessarily disadvantaged by long-term economic changes.

7. With respect to the increasingly complex and interlocking financial pressures which impinge upon the average individual today—taxes, savings, investments, retirement plans, insurance of all kinds, Social Security, property management, and estate planning, to mention but a few—we must play our proper role in devising workable and understandable mechanisms which will assist in reaching sound individual decisions. My guess is that the next phase of the computer revolution will be most evident in this connection. Home computers will become common-place; and, given expert help, families will be able to program their financial needs and requirements over the entire life cycle. There is much to be done. We face the social changes of the future with a sense of excitement and optimism. Unlike so many countries of the world which seem destined for long periods of agonizing revolution, we, thank heaven, have orderly means at our disposal for bringing about social change. Let us pray for the will to use them wisely and courageously.

Index